Whip the Cat

by Jan Mader
illustrated by Olivia Cole

Practice Decodable 40

McGraw Hill Education

Bothell, WA • Chicago, IL • Columbus, OH • New York, NY

MHEonline.com

Send all inquiries to:
McGraw-Hill Education
8787 Orion Place
Columbus, OH 43240

ISBN: 978-0-02-138907-0
MHID: 0-02-138907-1

Printed in China.

8 9 10 11 12 DSS 27 26 25 24 23

Gwen and Nick looked for Whip the cat.

"Which cat is Whip?" asked Nick.

“Whip is a tan cat. He has black spots,” said Gwen.

"He is called Whip? That is odd," said Nick.

"When Whip gets a whiff of snacks, he runs fast."

"It is not a whim. Whip runs fast for his snacks."